The little book of ROLLER SKATING

The little book of ROLLER SKATING

Written by

Illustrations by
Tasia Prince and Jess Rotter

CHRONICLE BOOKS
SAN FRANCISCO

Library of Congress Cataloging-in-Publication Data available.

ISBN 978-1-7972-1952-3

Manufactured in China.

MIX
Paper | Supporting responsible forestry
FSC™ C008047
FSC
www.fsc.org

Illustrations on pages 33, 42, 43, 44, 45, 47, 48, 49, 50, 51, 52, 57, 62, 63, 64, 66, 67, 68, 69, 70, 71, 73, 75, 76, 77, 79, 80, 81, 82, 89, 90, 91, 92, 93, 94, 119, 120, 212 by Tasia Prince.

Illustrations on pages 22, 26, 27, 29, 30, 31, 39, 60, 109, 111, 113, 114, 116, 122, 124, 125, 126, 133 by Jess Rotter.

Design by Evelyn Furuta.

10 9 8 7 6 5 4 3 2 1

CHRONICLE BOOKS
680 SECOND STREET
SAN FRANCISCO, CA 94107
WWW.CHRONICLEBOOKS.COM

THIS BOOK IS DEDICATED TO EVERYBODY WHO MAKES UP THE MOXI ROLLER SKATES STAFF AND COMMUNITY.

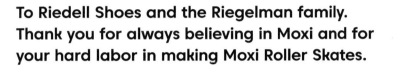

To Riedell Shoes and the Riegelman family. Thank you for always believing in Moxi and for your hard labor in making Moxi Roller Skates.

To the Moxi Roller Skates staff, made up of brave roller skaters who believe so much in the magic of roller skating, they dedicate their daily lives to it.

And to the inner children in all of us who always hoped we would live in a world full of adventure, love, and community. In honoring their dreams, we make the world a way better place for everyone!

CONTENTS

FOREWORD

This book was written by the team of roller skaters at Moxi Roller Skates. When I first started this company, there were very few roller skaters who worked to serve the industry. By teaching free lessons, organizing mass street skate events we call "roll outs," and showing customers how to use tools and customize their roller skate setups for specific uses, we built a community. With over twenty employees who are working their dream jobs, we're able to encourage others to make a lifestyle change and remind them that life is about adventure. Moxi is about dreaming, experiencing our connection to nature, and disconnecting from the monotony of everyday society—all things that we experience as children and yearn for as we get older. We are a true testament to togetherness, inspired by our inner child, who rides along with us on the magical toys we hope will one day become the shoes of the future.

So without further ado, welcome to roller skating! This book will serve as an introduction to it all. You will learn all the different ways there are to skate, all about the roller skate itself and its culture and community, and how roller skaters maintain a practice that is motivating, challenging, and fun!

—Michelle "Estro Jen" Steilen,

Founder of Moxi Roller Skates

INTRODUCTION

Get ready to grab your boom box and lace up your skates, because we are about to roll you through everything you need to know so that you and your roller skates have a wheely good time! Get familiar with your skates by exploring terminology, anatomy, types of skating, basic tricks, and so much more. Keep in mind that like other sports, risk is involved. Always take it slow and listen to your body. We will also dive into off-skate exercises and safety tips, as well as how to harness the motivation to lift yourself back up when you fall.

What are you waiting for? Let's ROLL!

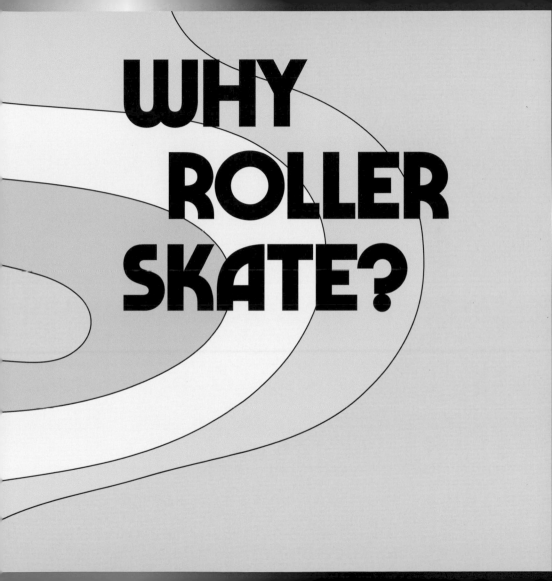

WHY ROLLER SKATE?

THERE ARE TOO MANY REASONS, SO WE'LL JUST LIST A FEW!

You feel like you're flying!

Since skating requires you to balance on wheels and glide across the earth powered by your own volition, there's a sense of presence with your body that makes you feel light, connected to the earth's gravitational pull.

Our favorite reason

It's good for your health!

Roller skating is a physical exercise, but unlike most aerobic or cardiovascular activities, it becomes more fun and peaceful the longer you do it. While skating can still be strenuous, often skaters say they don't feel like they are exercising at all!

For a sense of achievement!

Roller skating is inherently a risky activity, and skaters are always pushing the limits of their mind and physical body to learn new moves. Learning to roller skate is challenging, so landing a new move or even just getting the hang of balance gives many people a well-deserved sense of accomplishment.

You will make lots of new friends!

Roller skating promotes community and friendship! Skating together and exchanging new moves is the most common way to practice.

For rhythm and connection!

Roller skating and music go hand in hand. Whether you're touring a city with friends, skating for distance alone, dancing at the roller rink, or practicing in your driveway, music will loosen you up and motivate you to keep going. The beat helps you flow!

For peace!

Roller skating alone can focus your mind and allow you to feel in touch with your body, which in turn gives you a sense of relief and peace.

DID YOU KNOW?

According to a study conducted at the University of Massachusetts, when compared to running, skating causes less than 50 percent of the impact shock to joints. Other research studies show roller skating can improve not only balance but agility and coordination as well.

WHAT TO EXPECT AS A NEW SKATER

Practice Patience

If you're new to skating, or are even just trying something new on your usual skates, it might take your body some time to adjust. In the beginning, some movements can feel impossible. Give your body time to catch up to you, and you'll be amazed at how capable you really are.

Sore Muscles

You're activating your muscles in ways they have never experienced before. You may even take a few falls. Chances are you'll feel it the next day! Stretching and staying hydrated are always recommended to help prevent and regulate soreness.

Maintenance

Regular skate maintenance is a must. From tightening toe stops to cleaning bearings and rotating wheels, expect to get your hands dirty from time to time to ensure your skates are rolling properly. If you don't keep up with regular maintenance, there's a higher chance you'll have an accident. We'll get more into how to maintain your skates later on.

Growth and Plateaus

Your time and energy spent on skates will pay off! In time, you will become more comfortable on your skates, and eventually you may feel like pushing yourself beyond that. Whether that means tricks at the skate park, long-distance skating, or grooving at the roller rink, each new path you take will challenge you in different ways. It's important to remember that progress looks different for everyone and is not always linear.

THE FIT

Expect skates to fit snugly. Oftentimes, they feel tighter than your everyday shoes, and that's ideal! This prevents your foot from shifting in the boot as you skate and gives you more control.

Most importantly, expect to have a ton of FUN!

THE ROLLER SKATING COMMUNITY IS A DIVERSE ONE, FULL OF PEOPLE FROM ALL WALKS OF LIFE WHO ARE DIFFERENT AGES, SHAPES, AND SIZES.

With so many different ways to express yourself and so many people who are a part of the community, you can expect to meet others who share the same interests and passions as you. Roller skating with friends is a great way to support and bond with one another, bouncing ideas back and forth, all while enjoying the feeling of being on wheels.

HOW TO FIND SKATE FRIENDS

Social media is a great way to connect with other roller skaters in your community. There are skate crews all over the world that can help connect you to skaters nearby. One popular organization is CIB, which has chapters in most major cities. Stopping by your local skate park or roller rink or joining a Roller Derby league are also great ways to meet friends to skate with!

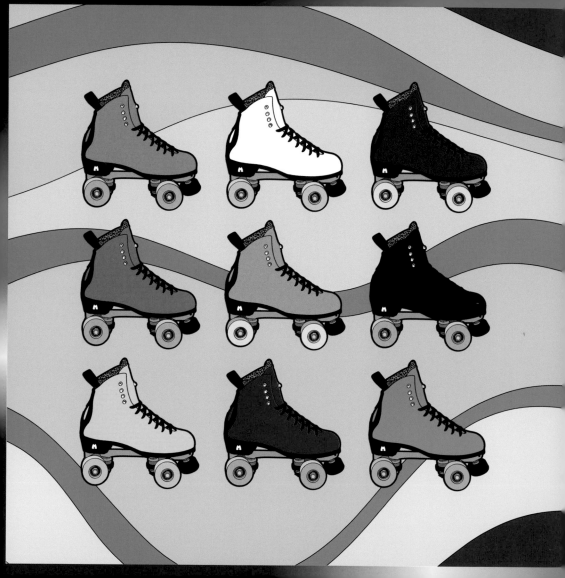

SKATE
ANATOMY

Your roller skate has many important components to be aware of:

Plate:
The plate is secured to the bottom of the boot and connects the boot to the trucks and wheels.

Boot:
The part you put your foot in!

Kingpin:
The kingpin goes through your plate and holds your trucks.

Pivot cup:
This is the small rubber cap that fits onto the pivot point of the truck and into the plate. It keeps your truck snug in place and prevents it from rubbing directly onto the plate.

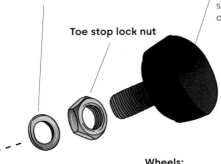

Toe stop washer

Toe stop lock nut

Toe stop: These are the breaks that sit at the front of your roller skate. There are different kinds of toe stops depending on the type of plate you have.

    a. Nonadjustable bolt-on toe stop: There is a screw that goes through the middle of the toe stop that attaches it to the plate. You cannot adjust the height placement of this style of toe stop.

    b. Adjustable toe stop: All Moxi Skates come with an adjustable toe stop. This uses a washer and lock nut to secure in place. You can adjust the toe stop height to your preference.

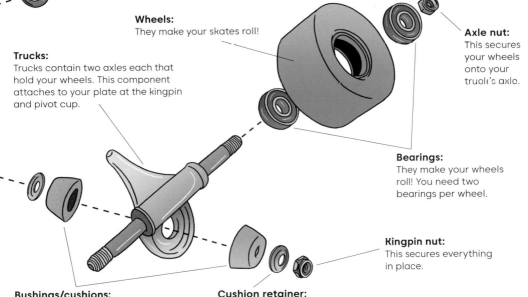

Wheels:
They make your skates roll!

Trucks:
Trucks contain two axles each that hold your wheels. This component attaches to your plate at the kingpin and pivot cup.

Axle nut:
This secures your wheels onto your truck's axle.

Bearings:
They make your wheels roll! You need two bearings per wheel.

Kingpin nut:
This secures everything in place.

Bushings/cushions:
Bushings, or cushions, are placed on the kingpin on either side of your trucks. Softer or harder bushings can change the way your skates feel.

Cushion retainer:
These are the cups that hold the cushions on the skate plates. Roller skate plate cushion cups are also referred to as cushion retainers. Retainers help distribute your weight more evenly across the whole cushion.

ANGLES MATTER!

Kingpins come in different degrees or angles that affect the nature of your skates' movement and how stable you may feel on them. A low number, like 10 degrees, is traditional and stable, with fast acceleration. A sharper angle, like 33 degrees, gives more agility and faster response in movement with a more forward, crouched stance.

BOOTS

Each type of skate is ideal for something different. While you can customize your plate, wheels, and other features to maximize function, let's first take a look at the boot! Some boots are better for the rink while some are better for the skate park, but these are recommendations—remember that you can skate anywhere with whichever boot you choose.

Suede high-top with heel:
recreation, rink, trails

Synthetic high-top with heel:
recreation, rink, trails

Suede high-top with heel and ankle support:
skate park, rink

Mid-top with internal heel and ankle support:
skate park, rink

Flat low-top:
Roller Derby, recreation

DIY build:
You can turn your shoes into skates! Park, street, and rink skaters are all known to build setups from shoes.

MATERIAL MATTERS!

Boot style is one thing, but the material the boot is made of also plays an important role in your skate's life. A boot made of suede or leather will last longer and withstand more falls without damaging the integrity of the skate. Suede skates can be soft and flexible, but when paired with added ankle support or padding, they make a solid outdoor and park skate. Skates that are made with synthetic materials often feel stiffer and may offer good ankle support. However, these boots may scrape or become damaged with too many falls, so they are best for indoor or recreational skating.

PLATES

When first starting out, you will most likely purchase a complete set with the plate already attached, so consider this when purchasing new skates. Sporting goods stores generally carry skates with cheap plastic hardware attached. Oftentimes, these plates are very light but are not durable and may break or react poorly to your movement, creating disconnect between you and your skates.

Not all plastic plates are bad, though. Many brands offer stronger nylon plates, which are lightweight and flexible, making them more durable and functional for many types of skating. An example of high quality nylon plates are the Powerdyne Nylon Thrust, found on our Lolly Complete Skates.

Metal plates are another option. Keep in mind that, just like with plastic plates, they are not all made equally. Generally, metal plates are stronger and more durable but have less flex, resulting in harder impact. They can be heavier than nylon, but some pricier metal plates can be extremely lightweight.

Every plate comes with kingpins that hold your trucks in place. Be aware that the degree of the kingpin will play a part in how your skates feel.

PLATES AND TOE STOPS

Lock Nut (15/16 in wrench)

Allen Key

Depending on the type of plate you have, the toe stop locking mechanism will vary. A lock nut is the most common locking mechanism and needs to be checked more frequently than Allen key locking systems to ensure that it is secure. An Allen key locking system prevents your toe stops from loosening as you skate! There are also bolt-on toe stops that utilize a screw in the center of the toe stop for security.

WHICH ROLLER SKATE ARE YOU?

I prefer neutrals

Mountains or the rain forest?

Are you more of a neutral-color person, or do you love color?

Give me color!

What's your favorite season?

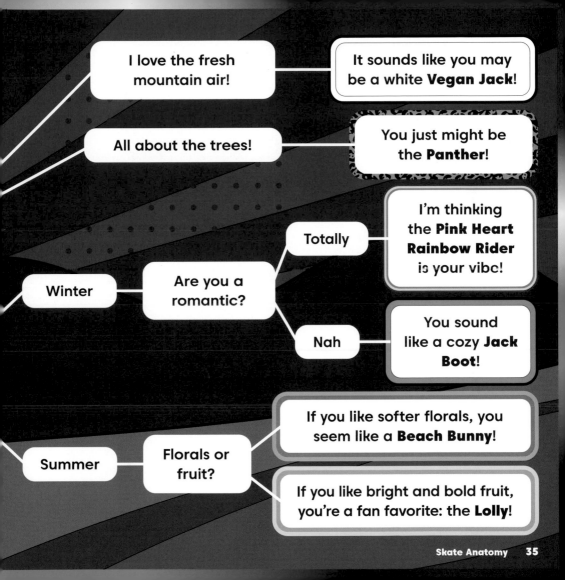

WHEELS

Wheels are the heart of the roller skate and can make a huge difference in the way you roll. Swapping out your wheels can transform your skates into a whole new ride. For a smooth ride on rough outdoor surfaces, grab a big soft wheel! To glide effortlessly across a smooth rink floor or skate park, go for something harder and smaller. Let's talk about what makes these wheels so different!

What makes a wheel?

Hardness, or durometer: This is noted by a number followed by an "a." The lower the number, the softer the wheel.

Size: This is the circumference of the wheel and is measured in millimeters (mm).

Width: This refers to the surface area that comes into contact with the ground.

BIG, SOFT WHEEL — 78A, 65 MM
Great for outdoor terrain like asphalt!

BIG, HARD WHEEL — 101A, 62 MM
Great for skating big bowls at
the skate park!

SMALL, HARD WHEEL — 103A, 52 MM
Great for skate park or rink, and
good for tricks like grinding!

**MID-SIZE, MODERATELY HARD WHEEL —
92A, 57 MM**
Hybrid wheel, great for going from street
to park! Also a good stepping stone for
transitioning from soft to hard wheels.

These are just a few examples of types of wheels you will see in the
wild and are some of our favorites, but there are so many brands
available and endless options to choose from.

DID YOU KNOW?

Until the 1970s, when skateboarders began to innovate their wheels for a better ride, the most common type of roller skate wheel was made from metal or clay. While in a friend's backyard, Frank Nasworthy saw some experimental urethane wheels on the friend's pair of roller skates. From there, he began developing the style of urethane wheels found in most skating disciplines today.

WHAT'S IN YOUR SKATE BAG?

LARGE TOTE/DUFFLE
Super prepared!
Y3 tool, helmet, pads, water bottle, extra axle nuts, extra toe stops, bearing tool, speaker, skate wax, snack, first aid kit

FANNY PACK
Just in case!
Vice Versa tool, extra axle nuts, wireless headphones, crab tool, bandages

Your bag could also include laces, stickers (for sticker slapping!), a camera, a tripod, and hand sanitizer.

SKATE MAINTENANCE

TOOLS

To stay rolling safely, tools are essential to keeping your skates properly adjusted and maintained throughout your adventures. Most skates use the following household tools for common adjustments:

Wheels: ½ in socket for axle nuts

Trucks: ⁹/₁₆ in socket for kingpin lock nuts

Lock nut toe stop: ¹⁵/₁₆ in wrench

Allen key toe stop: The size can vary depending on the brand of plate; however, a 5 mm Allen key will usually work.

You can also make maintenance even easier with these roller skate–specific tools:

A crab tool or Y3 for adjusting wheels, trucks, and toe stops with a lock nut

Y4 for adjusting wheels, trucks, and toe stops with an Allen key lock

And great to have on the go, the Moxi Vice Versa tool allows you to adjust any loose or wobbly wheels while on your roll out!

BEFORE LACING UP

Because roller skates have so many moving parts, it's always a good idea to make sure everything is adjusted to your liking before lacing up.

Some tips:

- Ensure your wheels are rolling freely but not wobbling from side to side.

- Make sure your toe stop is adjusted to your liking and tightly secured in place.

- Check that your trucks are all tightened/loosened equally to maintain balance.

CAUTION!

If you don't do regular maintenance, you may lose a toe stop, or even a wheel, mid-roll! It can happen to the best of us, but having a tool on hand will ensure you won't be stopped by hardware mishaps!

CLEANING BEARINGS

If your wheels no longer roll freely, or sound crunchy, it's time to clean or replace your bearings!

What you need: the dirty bearings, a container to hold your hardware and a container with a lid to clean the bearings in, paper towels, a safety pin or razor blade, bearing cleaner, bearing lube, and a bearing tool.

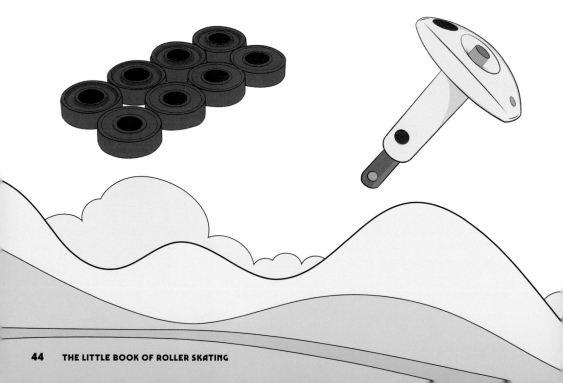

1. **Remove the bearings from the wheel and place the axle nuts in a container.**

   If using a bearing tool, press the button down and place the bearing tool inside the wheel, then release the button. The wheel should be able to spin freely on the tool. Pull the bearing out and press the button again to release.

2. **Use a safety pin or the edge of a razor blade to carefully remove the bearing covers.**

   Be careful not to puncture the bearing covers. Place the covers with the axle nuts.

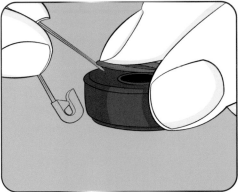

3. Place the dirty bearings inside another container and fill with bearing cleaner.

Place the lid on the container and shake the bearings around to release all the dirt. Let the bearings sit while you wipe down all the bearing covers and anything else that may be dirty.

4. Once clean, remove the bearings and tap any excess water out onto a paper towel.

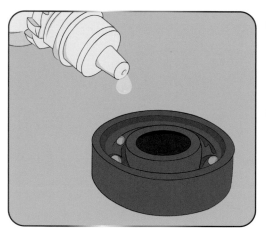

5. Allow the bearings to dry, then apply a couple drops of bearing lubricant to each bearing.

6. Place the bearing covers back on and spin each bearing to evenly distribute the lubricant.

7. Using your bearing tool, press the bearings back into the wheel.

Make sure they are pressed down evenly into the wheel hub so the bearings are flat, not crooked.

8. Put your wheels back on your skates, and now you're ready to roll—*smoothly*!

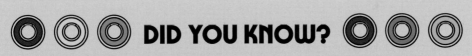

DID YOU KNOW?

If you don't have a bearing tool, you can use the axles on your trucks to remove or install your bearings. You can also install them by stacking two bearings on top of each other on the axle and pressing the wheel down to press the bearing into place.

CHANGING BUSHINGS

Bushings, or cushions, are found on either side of your trucks. Over time, they may wear down and need to be changed. You may notice cracking or crumbling, or that they have worn down and become smaller. You may also want to change your cushions to be softer or harder to make your skates more comfortable or reactive. Whatever your reason, here's a quick look at how to make this change.

1. Remove the kingpin nut and slide the trucks and old cushions off the axle.

Be sure to keep track of where each piece was so that you are able to put it back together!

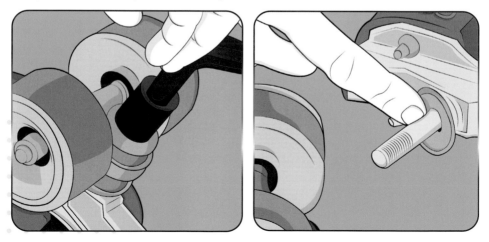

2. Discard the old cushions and slide the new ones onto the kingpin, sandwiching the truck.

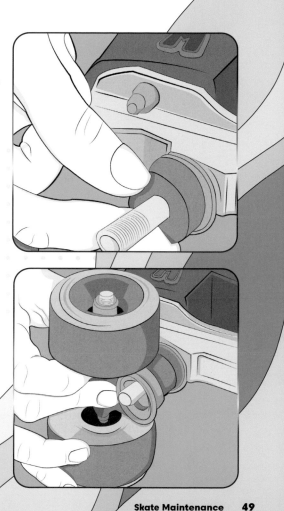

3. Secure the kingpin nut and adjust to the tightness you prefer.

Keep in mind, cushions break in over time. You may have to apply some pressure to get the kingpin nut back on.

CHECKING PIVOT CUPS

Pivot holes are where the arm of your truck sits. Inside each hole is a pivot cup. This prevents the truck from rubbing against the plate and causing damage. Over time, your pivot cups will eventually break. Always check up on these parts to prevent a more expensive fix. When you notice you have a broken pivot cup, here's what to do!

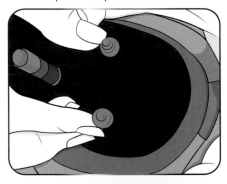

1. **Remove the kingpin nut, trucks, and cushions and place them to the side.**

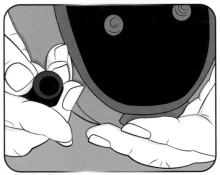

2. **Remove the old and broken pivot cups.**

   If it is lodged in there, you may need to use a screwdriver to wedge it out.

3. **Replace with a new pivot cup, put the trucks and cushions back on, and secure the kingpin nut.**

CHANGING AND ROTATING TOE STOPS

Toe stops are super important, seeing as you rely on them to stop you when needed. Once you master the toe stopping technique, you will probably find that you favor one foot over the other. If one toe stop is looking worn down, try rotating it with the other to wear them out evenly. Once both of your toe stops are worn down, it's time for some new ones!

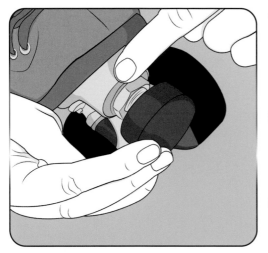

1. **Remove your old toe stops using the corresponding tool.**

   If you're unsure which tool to use, check out page 42!

2. **If your plate requires a lock nut, remove the washer and nut from the old toe stop and place them onto the new one.**

3. **Screw the lock nut onto the toe stop up to the position you want your toe stop to be in.**

4. **Screw the toe stop back into place until the lock nut reaches the plate.**

5. **With the toe stop in place, tighten the nut or Allen lock securely.**

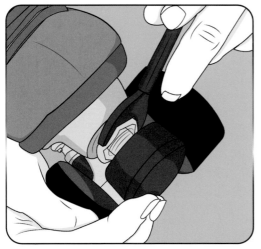

LONG STEM VS. SHORT STEM: WHICH TOE STOP IS BEST FOR YOU?

It's a preference! Long stem toe stops place your toe stop closer to the ground, while short stem toe stops are able to screw all the way up to the plate. Short stem toe stops are usually preferred once you're more comfortable on your skates.

LOOSE VS. TIGHT TRUCKS

Don't forget to check your trucks! They can become too loose or uneven over time. To check that all four trucks are tightened equally, look at the thread or set your skates on the ground to see if all four wheels rest evenly. If they're looking loose, adjusting your trucks is so easy! Simply loosen or tighten the kingpin lock nut to your liking.

Experiment with your setup to find what best suits your style of skating. You can adjust your trucks by loosening or tightening the truck nut.

- **Loose:** Turns and movements will come more easily when you shift your weight. Overall, loose trucks are more responsive to your movements.

- **Tight:** Turns and movements will require more effort and weight distribution. However, tight trucks will provide you with more stability.

ROTATING WHEELS!

Just like with cars, it's always a good idea to rotate your wheels! Depending on how you skate, you may find that you wear out the edges of some wheels more than others. To make your wheels work for you longer, rotate them so that they wear evenly.

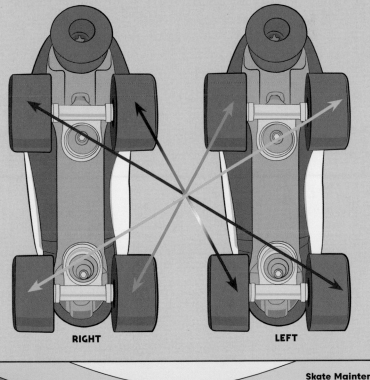

RIGHT   LEFT

PROTECTIVE GEAR

Protective gear, your body's new best friend! Much like tools to keep your skates rolling safely, protective gear is a must to keep YOU rolling safely.

Protecting your knees, head, wrists, and elbows will help prevent injury and have you feeling confident as you learn a new skill. Nowadays, protective gear comes in many different patterns and designs so you can express your individual style! Other protective gear can include mouth guards, shin guards, knee gaskets, and even BUTT PADS! Don't hesitate to pad up to the max, or whatever makes you feel good.

IT HAPPENS!

While accidental falls can take us by surprise, you can also practice mindful falling with the help of your protective gear. Check out page 78 to see how you can best utilize your kneepads and other gear to take control of your falls!

BEGINNER SKILLS

Standing Up

When you first get your skates on, step one is standing up!

If you are sitting on a chair or a bench, place your feet beneath your knees in a V-shape with your heels together. Press up to stand, keeping your chest over your toes so that you do not fall back.

If you are sitting on the ground, first get onto your knees and step your strong foot out. Then, using your knee for stability, press yourself up.

Once you are standing, keep in mind that your body should always be in alignment to prevent falls. Keep your chest, knees, and toes stacked on top of one another.

While holding on to something if needed, practice putting all your weight onto one foot and then switching to the other. Then, practice putting all your weight onto the ball of your foot to walk on your toe stops. Getting comfortable holding weight on each foot separately is important because when you start to stride forward, you will be shifting your weight back and forth to gain momentum.

LACING

If your skates aren't feeling secure, try some different lacing techniques!

HEEL SLIPPING

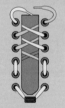

TOE PAINS

TOO TIGHT ON TOP

ONE AREA TOO TIGHT

WIDE FOREFOOT

WIDE FEET IN GENERAL

HIGH MIDFOOT

HIGH ARCHES

NARROW FEET

NARROW HEEL + WIDE FOREFOOT

FLAT FEET

SWOLLEN FEET

SKATING FORWARD

Once you've stood up, try skating forward!

Striding

With the body in alignment, place feet hip width apart. Start by doing a "penguin walk," shifting your weight back and forth to move forward. Once you are comfortable with this movement, begin to slightly stagger your feet one in front of the other, still hip-width apart. While holding weight on one foot, use the other to push through the ball of your foot in a sideways motion. Then switch feet.

Crossovers

Once you feel comfortable with your stride, you can work up to crossovers. Keeping the body aligned over the foot that is holding your weight, take your other foot and cross it over in front of your weight-bearing foot. Apply pressure through the crossed foot, and push through that foot as it comes back behind you to bear weight. Once your weight has transferred, switch to cross over the other foot in front of you. You can do this both backward and forward!

STOPPING

Now you know how to roll, so let's learn how to stop!

Plow Stop

One easy way to stop is by using your leg muscles! With your feet under you, squeeze your thighs as you push your toes and feet into a wider stance. Keep your thighs engaged to create resistance as you scoop your feet back under you with your toes pointing together. It's much like drawing a big circle on the ground with your toes leading.

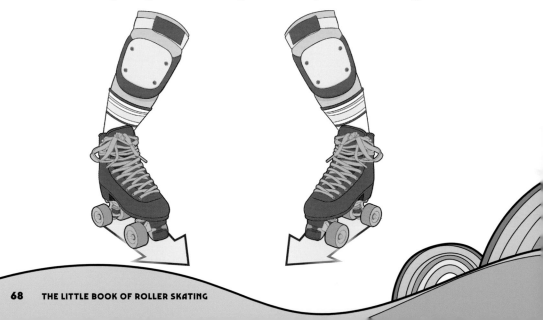

Toe Stop Drag

Another way to stop is by dragging a toe stop. With your body aligned, bearing weight on one foot, carefully allow the loose foot to go behind you. Point your toe stop down and press it into the ground while pulling it forward to meet the weight-bearing foot.

CAUTION!

When dragging a toe stop, be sure that you are applying the right amount of pressure as you scoop the dragging foot forward. Without proper pressure, your toe stop may stick rather than drag you to a slow and safe stop.

T-Stop

The T-stop is one of the most common ways to stop! However, it is more difficult than a plow stop and toe stop drag. Much like the toe stop drag, you will start by bearing your weight onto one foot. Position your other foot behind your front foot at a 90-degree angle. Keeping most of your weight on your front foot, apply pressure to your back foot wheels as you pull your back foot toward your front foot to stop. Depending on what feels best to you, you can apply the pressure to either your front two wheels, inside wheels, or outside wheels to T-stop.

90°

Turn Around Toe Stop

Turn around toe stops are the fastest and most effective way to stop on a dime! Fair warning: For this stop, you will need to be able to do either a 180 jump or a forward to backward transition. While skating forward, transition to backward by scooping your front foot around while your back foot follows, putting you in a backward skating position. At fast speeds, you will need to jump into a backward position to prevent momentum taking you down. Once you are in a backward position, lunge into the ball of your back foot, pressing the toe stop into the ground.

TURNING AROUND

Another important skill you may want to learn is transitioning from forward to backward. It is a necessary building block for other skills. Let's get into it!

Opening the Book

While skating forward, bring one foot in front, pointing your toes forward. With your weight on the front foot, allow your back foot to lift so that you are in a sideways stance with the toes of both feet facing out. With your weight still on your front foot, bring the heel of your back foot toward you. Once your back foot is under you, transfer your weight to it. Then lift (or scoop) your front foot to go in front of you once again, turning your head and shoulders as this happens. Once completed, you will be moving backward. Don't forget to always turn your head and shoulders to face the direction you are traveling!

Once you've learned how to do a 180 jump, you can also jump to transition from forward to backward! We will talk more about jumping later on.

SKATING BACKWARD

Now that you have transitioned to a backward stance, it's time to learn how to keep the momentum! Skating backward is the same as skating forward . . . but backward! It may feel uncomfortable or awkward at first, but stick with it. Your muscle memory will build, and before you know it, it will feel just as easy as skating forward.

Bubbles

Creating bubbles can help you gain some movement from a nonmoving, backward position. This is a great exercise for building comfort and confidence. Start by turning your head and shoulders to look behind you with your feet in a wide, slightly staggered position. Use your heels to draw circles on the ground, bringing them out and in as you engage your thighs, scooping yourself backward. Once you are comfortable with this, you can deepen your stagger and do the same bubbles, but with one foot behind you and one foot in front, nearly crossing them as they come to the center. You can even begin to switch your back and front feet as you create bubbles, making a backward crossover stride.

You can also use one foot to move yourself backward! Put most of your weight on your front foot while allowing your back skate's front two wheels to gently draw S-shapes on the ground behind you. This gentle movement creates a ton of energy with very little effort and is a great way to maintain the speed you already have from transitioning forward to backward.

Edges

Edges are a very important aspect of skating—you likely already use your edges without even knowing it! Being aware and in control of your edges will allow you to build your skills and help you create more power and fluid movements.

WHAT ARE EDGES?

Edges have to do with your wheels. Your skates have three edges: the outer edge, the inner edge, and the middle, or center, edge.

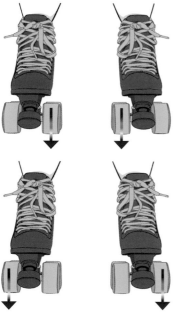

You are on your inside edges when your weight is on your inner two wheels with your knee hovering in past your foot and the bottom of your skate facing away from you. You should feel pressure as the inside of your foot presses against the boot.

You are on your outside edges when your weight is on your outside wheels with your knee hovering over your pinky toe and the bottom of your skate angled toward you. You should feel pressure as the outside of your foot presses against the boot. Remember to keep your upper body over your foot to maintain balance.

You are on your middle, or center, edges when you are on all four wheels equally.

EXERCISE!

While standing with your chin up and body in alignment, practice shifting to each edge, one foot at a time. You can leave the other foot down for balance, trying not to put weight on it. Shift one foot from edge to edge, and then switch to the other foot.

Once you've found your balance, start recognizing the use of your edges and lean more into them. Two ways you may already be using your edges are by turning and striding.

FALLING

Let's get humble: Falling is a big part of skating. It's inevitable, so instead of feeling discouraged, treat each fall as a learning experience! It's how we learn from our mistakes, how we progress, and how we are able to laugh at ourselves from time to time that make us better skaters. There is nothing to be embarrassed about when it comes to falling because we *all* do it. It can seem scary, but there are a few techniques for making falling a bit safer.

IMPORTANT TIP!

The smaller you can make yourself, the smaller the fall. For example, if you are standing straight up and take a fall, there will be a greater impact than if you were closer to the ground. You always want to get low before you fall to lighten the impact, so try getting a nice bend in your knees and waist.

Taking a Knee

You should only do this with kneepads on! Bend your knees to brace for impact, and drop one of your knees to the ground, as if you're doing a lunge.

Taking a Hip/Falling Backward

A common way many beginners fall is straight backward onto their butt. You may find that if you stand up too straight and lose your balance, your skates want to slip out from under you, and your instinct is to fall back. Whenever possible, you want to avoid falling straight back onto

your butt because you have a greater chance of injuring your tailbone, your head, or even your wrists. Instead, try turning your body to the side to catch yourself with your hip and the side of your leg. This will decrease the chance of hitting your head or putting too much impact on your tailbone.

Falling Forward

Big surprise! Falling forward is going to be all about getting low! If you feel yourself tripping forward or you need to brace yourself for a fall, you want to get as low as you can, pick a side to fall onto, and absorb the impact with the side of your butt and leg.

More of a visual learner? Check out our YouTube channel!

"Our greatest glory is not in never falling, but in rising every time we fall."
—Confucius

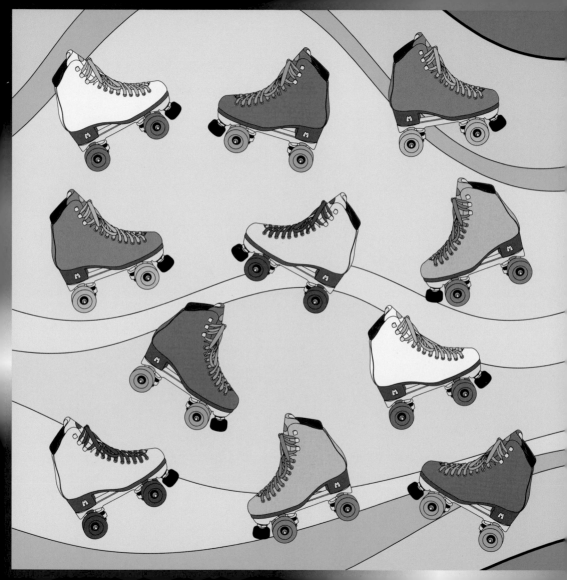

EQUIPMENT

For outdoor skating, you will most likely want wheels that are softer, or lower in durometer. Softer wheels can roll over rough surfaces, cracks, and various debris much easier than hard wheels. See page 37 for our wheel guide! When skating outdoors, there can be small obstacles or terrain variants that may occasionally trip you up, so be sure to choose safety gear that you feel most comfortable wearing.

Safety Precautions

Skating outdoors on streets and sidewalks requires caution and awareness. There may be cracks you could trip over, abrupt changes in terrain, traffic, and pedestrians! Be sure you are aware of your surroundings at all times. Use proper etiquette when passing others, and obey stop signs and traffic lights.

TERRAIN

Outdoor terrain can vary quite a bit, sometimes even depending on where you live! You might have sand, gravel, smooth pavement, rough pavement, sidewalks, curbs, or tactile paving. Typically, a soft wheel and good skate form can get you rolling over most of these terrain types, but we have a few tips that could help when dealing with certain obstacles.

Domes and Pavers

Have you ever noticed those bumpy patterns at the end of sidewalks before an intersection? They're called truncated domes and detectable warning pavers. They help the visually impaired detect when they are about to leave the sidewalk and enter the street. Although domes and pavers have a great purpose and certainly shouldn't be removed, they can be tricky to maneuver on skates. We always recommend bending at the knees when rolling over rough areas, and lifting a little bit of your weight off your toes and onto your heels. This will help you roll over these obstacles more efficiently. Whenever possible, you also want to try taking the route with the fewest bumps to roll over.

Curbs

When stepping off a curb, you want to take your weight off the foot that is closest to the street and set it down into the street. You will then transfer your weight onto that foot and push off with the other to give yourself some momentum. Once you have successfully stepped off the curb and into the street, you can regain your regular skate posture. When stepping up a curb, you can hop with both feet if you feel comfortable and confident enough to do so, or you can step up one foot at a time with controlled speed. The technique would be similar to stepping off, but you will lift the foot closest to the ledge and transfer weight from one foot to the other until you can regain posture.

Stairs

You may find yourself needing to get up or down stairs. We find the best way to accomplish this is to either side step up/down the steps or walk on your toe stops:

And if there is a railing accessible that could assist you, certainly feel free to use it!

Hills and Slopes

Heading down a hill or slope can be rather intimidating. Fear not! There are a couple drills you can practice that will get you comfy going downhill.

Slaloming, or carving, is one way to slow down and gain control on hills. This technique is similar to skiing, where you shift your weight from side to side while pointing your knees and toes toward the direction of your carve.

Another option would be to roll backward, using your toe stop as a brake for speed control.

DO YOU HEAR THAT?

Occasionally, you may hear some rattling or squeaking coming from your skate. If this happens to you, you'll want to check your wheels and toe stops. A loose wheel or toe stop nut could be the cause of this rattling. A seized bearing can also squeak. If your wheels cannot freely spin, it may be time to clean or replace your bearings! Check out page 44 for a how-to!

TRICKS FOR BEGINNERS

These tricks are general beginner tricks that can be done anywhere, even on grass or carpet, for a safe and fun learning experience!

Shoot the Duck 📷

To nail this trick, you'll want to practice your squats and getting low. Drop your hips as low as they will go so that all your weight and balance is coming from your hip flexors and feet. Once you are able to get to the right level, you can shift your weight onto one foot while extending out the opposite leg. You can grab your skate or leg for some extra flair too! To get back up, just follow the steps in reverse. We like to practice this on grass first to find the right balance and trust in the drop.

Jumps

Learning to jump can come in handy for many different reasons, but jumps are also just fun! Before you get into any jumps, be sure you feel steady and comfortable rolling on skates first. Make sure your legs are warmed up—try doing some squats. A good jump is always powered through the legs. From there you want to carry your arms up for momentum, flick off the ground with your toes while extending your legs, and absorb the landing by squatting back down and sitting back in your hips. Once you have this down, you can begin adding rotations like 180s and 360s!

360 Jumps

Rotations come from adding a twist in your shoulders and hips while jumping. Find a spot on the ground in front of you or on a wall across from you to focus on. Focusing on this spot will help you rotate all the way around. Start in your squat position, slightly wind up through the arms, pull them in while following through with your shoulders, flick off the ground with your toes, find your spot, and absorb the landing. This may take some practice, but don't give up on it!

Manuals

Manuals are when you lift some of your wheels up while still riding on the others. Manuals have many variations, but they all require balance! They can be done with both feet or just one. You can practice these on carpet or grass to get a feel for the balance before you add some speed to it.

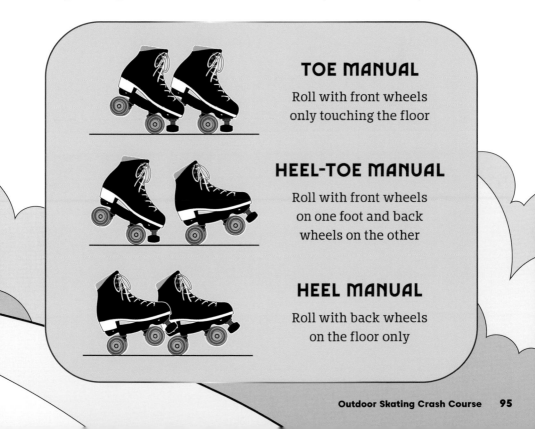

TOE MANUAL

Roll with front wheels only touching the floor

HEEL-TOE MANUAL

Roll with front wheels on one foot and back wheels on the other

HEEL MANUAL

Roll with back wheels on the floor only

Everyone needs a break from time to time. Listen to your body and rest as needed. Even when we aren't rolling, there are many ways to keep working on our skills and strengthen our bodies. Take time off as an opportunity to work on skate maintenance, stretch, set new skate goals, plan a skate event, watch videos for inspiration, participate in community outreach, or even spend time on other hobbies you may have! You just might find some of your skater friends share similar interests. We're always inspired by the creativity of skaters on and off their wheels.

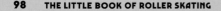

OFF-SKATE PRACTICE

Many of the tricks and skills done on skates can also be practiced off skates! If you feel like you are struggling with a particular skill or want to be sure you are practicing good form, give it a try in your shoes! Off-skate practices are not only good for building skills but they're also great for keeping our bodies healthy so that we can keep rolling as long as we'd like!

Exercises

SQUATS

Squats are the perfect exercise for solidifying good skating form and safe falls. They are also great for strengthening your legs, and you'll need strong legs for many of the skills you may try on your skates.

SIT-UPS AND PLANKS

Most often, we do not pay attention to how crucial a solid core is in skating. Your core is your body's powerhouse. It keeps you stable, aids in common movements in skating, and gives you good posture. It would be a disservice to neglect your powerhouse! There are many abdominal exercises out there, but to start, you can try these!

Basic Sit-Ups

Bicycle Crunches **Planks**

LUNGES

Much like squats, lunges are an excellent exercise because we use our legs so much in skating. Lunges actually mimic several skating movements.

Basic Lunge:
great for balance and control!

Curtsy Lunge:
great for crossovers!

Side Lunge:
great for strides!

PUSH-UPS

You may have already discovered—or will be surprised to find out—just how much we use our arms in skating! They help us with our balance and getting up off the ground, and are crucial for some more advanced skills, like handstands at the park or floor work at the rink!

YOGA AND STRETCHING

Stretching is very important when it comes to keeping our bodies healthy for skating. When we work our muscles and tire out our physical bodies, stretching is what helps restore us. Having elasticity in our muscles and joints decreases the chances of injury and fatigue. There are endless ways to stretch, but we thought we would give you this fun yoga sequence to try!

You certainly are not limited to yoga, so feel free to find ways to stretch that are fitting for you! There are certain muscle groups that we tend to work the most while we skate, such as glutes, hamstrings, quads, hip flexors, abdominals, and ankles. Be sure to pay special attention to those areas.

TYPES OF SKATING

There are so many ways to enjoy your skates! Here are a few of the more popular ways people enjoy rolling. Try one or try them all—it's up to you!

FITNESS/RECREATIONAL

You certainly don't have to fly off ramps or get into technical footwork just to be a roller skater! Not everyone is looking to bust out dance moves or do crazy tricks. One of the most common ways people use roller skates is by just getting out there and cruising. Fitness or recreational skating can be so many things. The world is your skate oyster! You can cruise on city sidewalks, countryside bike trails, sunny beach paths, or any surface where skating is permitted. Long-distance skating, exploring trails, and participating in roll outs in your town are all great ways to enjoy skating while exercising or socializing. Whether you're a beginner or at a more expert level, the outdoors is always for you!

DID YOU KNOW?

Skateboarding was actually invented by taking trucks off roller skates and attaching them to a board. Once skateboarders started taking their skills to pools and bowls in the '70s, roller skaters began doing the same!

RINK

If you love moving to the music with a smooth surface to groove on, throw on your favorite outfit and head down to your local skating rink! Rink skating has been a staple for decades. Most people lace up their first pair of rental skates at their local roller rink as a young child. From creating childhood memories to building a lifelong love affair, the roller rink provides a smooth surface to glide, dance, and catch a break from everyday life.

DIFFERENT CITY, DIFFERENT STYLE

There is a long history of Black culture in roller skating, especially in the rink scene. Over the years, many cities formed their own signature styles of skating that were unique to their area. For example, roller skaters from Chicago are known for a style called "JB," or James Brown style.

New to the Rink?

GEAR YOU NEED

If you're just starting out, softer wheels may feel more comfortable. Eventually, you'll want to upgrade your wheels to something a bit harder. Check out our wheel guide on page 37! You might notice many skaters at the rink appear to have no toe stops. They're actually using jam plugs! These are small plastic inserts that replace your typical rubber toe stop. It allows skaters to do specific movements and dances.

ETIQUETTE

Faster skaters usually cruise on the outside areas of the rink floor; slower skaters stay on the inside. Some skaters will practice their moves or have a jam circle in the middle of the floor to stay out of the way of others. Always be sure to respect those around you, be aware of your surroundings, and follow the rink rules. Ditch the headphones and vibe with others!

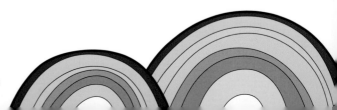

Beginner Spins

Spins can be done with your heel or toe. You can either use just your heels, just your front wheels, or one foot. Spins can be stylized in so many different ways. Get creative with it!

CHOREOGRAPHY

You might see some synchronized footwork out on the rink. There are so many variations of rollerdance—so many things you can learn!

Interested in learning more about rollerdance? Ask your rink if they offer classes, or look online for rollerdance or jam skating tutorials.

DID YOU KNOW?

Richard Humphrey, who has been skating for over sixty years, coined the term *rollerdance*! To hear his story, check out this video!

SKATE PARK

Roller skating at a skate park is becoming more and more popular! Just as skateboarders or in-line skaters utilize the skate park to drop in, carve bowls, catch air, or do coping tricks, you can learn to do all that on your roller skates! Unlocking new tricks and skills on unique obstacles is not only fun, it's also gratifying.

New to the Skate Park?

1, 2 & 3: Quarter Pipes

4: Quarter Pipe with Vert (need to make the top of it more vertical)

5: Ledge or Grind Box

6: Flat Rail or Bar

7: Pyramid

8: Down Ledge

9: Mini Ramp

10: Kicker Ramps

GEAR YOU NEED

Typically, skaters prefer smaller, harder wheels for the park, rather than softer outdoor wheels. Harder wheels allow you to perform better grinds, and they give you more agility and speed. You will want to pad up with full gear when beginning your park journey! Skate park skating is a high-risk activity, so always be sure to wear protection to your comfort level. As you progress, you may want to look into grind blocks and wide trucks. Grind blocks are made from various plastic materials. They sit between your trucks and are designed to help you with grinds and slides on coping, rails, and ledges. They can even assist you with stalls. Though neither are required for park skating, they can expand your bag of tricks!

ETIQUETTE

Although the skate park is a fun and creative place to skate, there are still guidelines to follow. Always be aware of others at the park. Pay attention to others' run patterns to avoid bumping into anyone. Be sure you are sharing the space with others and taking turns. Sometimes when we are starting out, it may take us some extra time on an obstacle to get comfortable. If other people at the park want to use the same obstacle, just be sure that you are mindful of how long you are using it so they may also have a turn.

Beginner Park Tips and Tricks

SKATING DOWN A BANK

If you are new to the park, a good place to begin is learning to roll down a bank. Banks can range in steepness, so look for something a bit more mellow to start. Like always, you will want to practice good form! Keep your feet staggered and your knees bent. You should feel almost like you are doing a squat but with a slight lean forward to brace for the decline. You can use your arms as extra balance in front of you. You will gain speed as you roll down, so be prepared to slow down after the obstacle if needed.

PUMPING

Pumping a ramp feels similar to swinging on a swing. You want to pump with your legs at the right moments to create momentum. Start with your feet slightly staggered and your knees slightly bent. When creating a pump, you want to bend deeper in the knees and sit at the waist. Pumps should happen at the start of the transition of a ramp and on the way back down the transition. You would repeat this backward if skating on a mini ramp. When skating backward, be sure to look behind you.

STALLING

Stalling is what we call getting your feet planted on the coping of a ramp. To do this, you should feel comfortable pumping the entirety of the ramp first and rolling back in backward. You can even practice this on a ledge or curb to get the feel for what stalls are like. Eventually, you can even do ledge slides.

STREET

Street skating, like skate park skating, takes inspiration from skateboarding and in-line skating. Street skating is about getting creative and utilizing the world around you as your skate park—respectfully. From jumping stairs and grinding ledges, rails, or parking blocks to stalling curbs and airing gaps, street skating is whatever you make it.

DID YOU KNOW?

Michelle Steilen was the first roller skater featured in a Bones Bearings video in 2013. Watch it here!

Released in 2019, "Street Fighters" was the first full-length street video featuring roller skaters from all over the world. Watch it here!

OTHER TYPES OF SKATING

Roller Derby

Roller Derby is a team sport and is usually full contact. It was started in the 1930s, died down a bit, was then revived in the early 2000s, and is still an active sport today! If you are interested in joining a Roller Derby team, you can learn more about the sport and check for local teams on the WFTDA® website.

Speed Skating

Speed skating is a competition style of roller skating that can be done solo or as a team. This style of skating requires specific skates, gear, and skills. It is typically done on an oval track.

Artistic Skating

Artistic skating is very similar to figure ice-skating, but on roller skates! If you are interested in learning more about this facet of skating, check out your local roller rink to see if they offer lessons.

WHAT TYPE OF SKATER ARE YOU?

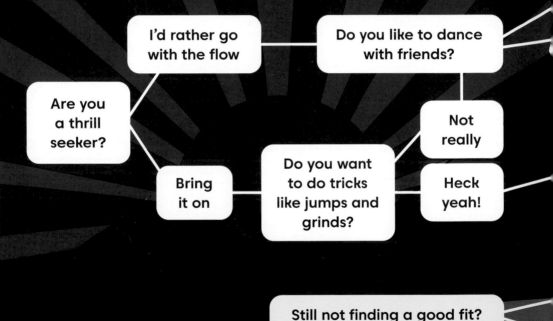

I'd rather go with the flow

Do you like to dance with friends?

Are you a thrill seeker?

Not really

Bring it on

Do you want to do tricks like jumps and grinds?

Heck yeah!

Still not finding a good fit?

Crank the tunes!

I'd check out the **rink** if I were you!

I just wanna roll

Recreational skating might be where it's at for you!

Do you want to "surf" the concrete?

Yes!

Skate park skating sounds like your thing!

Nah

You might be a **street skater**!

I'd prefer a team-style sport

Roller Derby could be for you!

Format training full of grace and balance is more my jam

Sounds like you'd enjoy **artistic skating** classes!

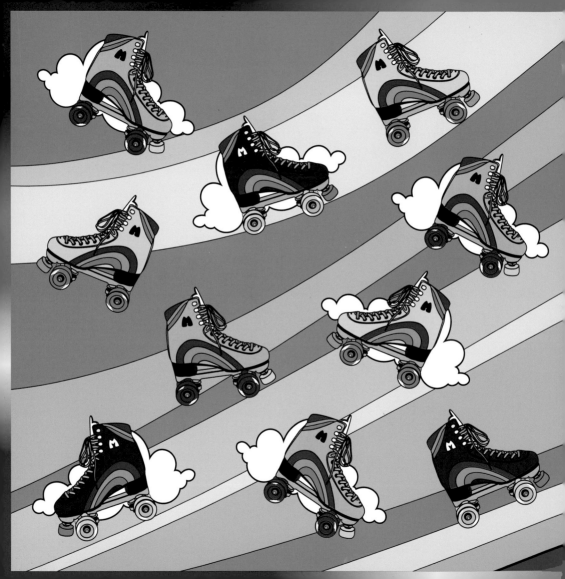

There are no rules! When it comes to how to dress when skating, you should wear what makes you feel good! However, here are a few tips you may find helpful:

TIP 1:

When roller skating outside, you want to be seen! That's why you'll see a lot of roller skaters wearing brightly colored clothing.

TIP 2:

While roller skating, risks are unavoidable! That is why we wear protective gear and clothing that we are okay with falling in.

TIP 3:

Roller skating can really make us break a sweat! Breathable, moisture-wicking materials are most comfortable. Avoiding bulky clothing will also allow your arms and legs to move more freely.

CUSTOMIZE AND ACCESSORIZE

There are endless ways to customize your skates so that they fully embody your personality! There are laces in almost every color and design, different-colored toe stops, toe covers, light-up wheels, and so much more! You can even paint or dye your skates! The possibilities are endless.

HERE ARE SOME DIY TIPS:

⭐ Our favorite brand of suede dye and paints is Angelus Direct.

⭐ You can use fabric dye to change the color of your wheels.

⭐ Check out your local craft store for beads, charms, or other supplies to build your own custom accessories!

CUSTOMIZE YOUR OWN SKATE!

Before committing to the real thing, use these pages to sketch out your ideas!

The roller skate community is expansive! If you're looking to meet other roller skaters and find your local community, most crews have social media accounts or Facebook groups. These groups will occasionally host meetups, which are the perfect opportunity to meet new people! And if you are not able to find any skate groups in your area, you can certainly start one. It might take some time to build a crew in your community, but skating with others and making new friends is so worth it.

CONCLUSION

We hope this book was able to offer you a bit of confidence and knowledge to help you get started. We are so excited that you have decided to begin your skate journey with us! We would love for you to stay in touch. We host skate camps, teach classes, host challenges and meetups, and create skate tutorials online for your pleasure. Thank you so much for all your support!

Follow us for even more fun content at **@moxirollerskates** on Instagram and YouTube!

Moxi Roller Skates was founded by Michelle Steilen, whose dream was to create a rainbow of roller skates that would encourage as many people as possible to get on eight wheels. Riedell is our family-owned-and-operated manufacturer, who makes our skates by hand with true care. We really believe that roller skates are the shoes of the future, and we are so excited you have joined us on this journey!